Hello!

Illustrated by
Tony Flowers

Yiasou!
Sawatdi kha!
Ciao!
Apa kabar?
Hello!
Midh!
Ni hao!
Marhaba!
Nhinhi-ka patha thanam?
Annyong!
Niina marni?
Xin chao!
Konnichiwa!

Hello!

We're learning about different cultures. We all speak English but many of us can speak another language too.

My name is Ivy.

My family comes from Badu Island in the Torres Strait.

I speak Kala Lagaw Ya.

Midh!
Hello!

I love eating akul.

(mangrove mussels)

Sometimes I watch my aka make wakul out of palm leaves.

(grandmother)

(mats)

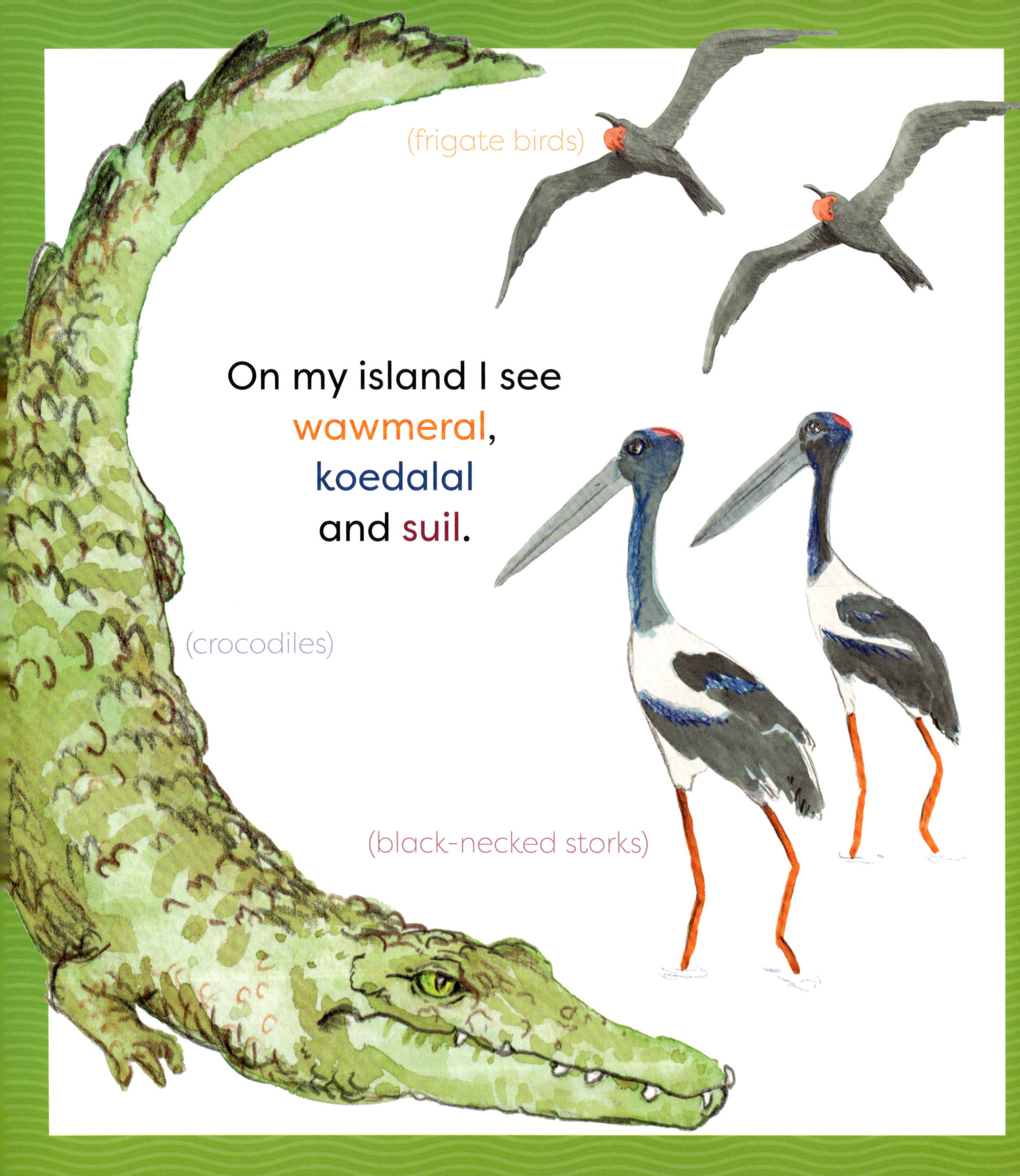

On my island I see
wawmeral,
koedalal
and suil.

On special days I perform Gumi Rangadh.

(a traditional dance)

I wear a zazi and selal.

(shells)

I like listening to the story about how the warrior, Thagay, became stars in the sky.

urapun
1

ukasar
2

koeyma
3/many

My name is **Hua**.
My family comes from China.
I speak Chinese.

I love eating shui jiao
水饺

(dumplings)

and zong zi.
粽子

(sticky rice
in bamboo leaves)

On special days
I wear my qi pao
旗袍
(traditional dress)

and I fly my
feng zheng.
风筝

yi	er	san	si	wu
一	二	三	四	五
1	2	3	4	5

I'm learning
wu shu.
武术

(martial arts)

Every week I practise
min jian wu dao.
民间舞蹈

(Chinese folk dancing)

liu	qi	ba	jiu	shi
六	七	八	九	十
6	7	8	9	10

My name is **Nikos**.
My family comes from Greece.
I speak Greek.

Yiasou!
Γειασου
Hello!

I love eating **souvlaki**

σουβλακι

(grilled meat on a skewer)

and **melomakarono.**

μελομακαρονο

(honey biscuits)

On special days I wear my **foustanella** φουστανελλα

(traditional dress)

(a Greek dance)

and I perform **kalamatianos.** καλαματιανος

ena	dio	tria	tessera	pente
ενα	δυο	τρια	τεσσερα	πεντε
1	2	3	4	5

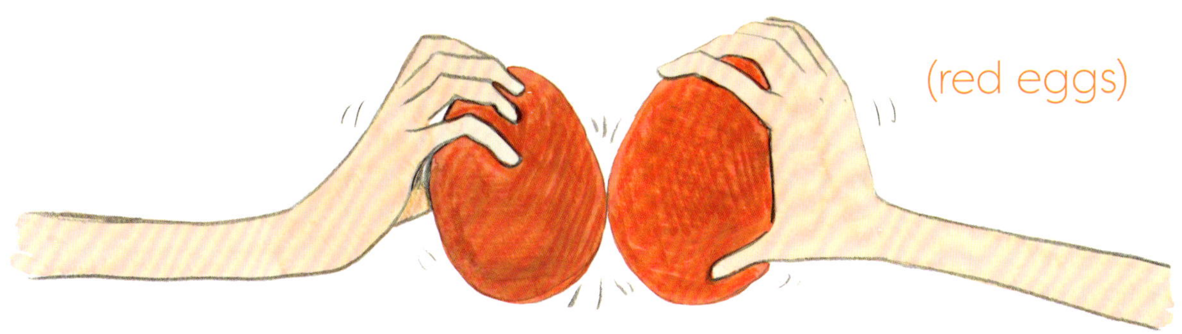

(red eggs)

At Easter we tap kokkina avga together.
κοκκινα αυγα

My favourite song is 'Ax Kounelaki'.
Αχ Κουνελακι

('Little Rabbit')

Yiasou!
Γειασου
Goodbye!

eksi	efta	okto	enia	deka
εξι	εφτα	οκτω	εννια	δεκα
6	7	8	9	10

My name is **Budi**.
My family comes from Indonesia.
I speak Indonesian.

Apa kabar?
How are you?

I love eating nasi goreng

(fried rice)

and gado-gado.

(salad with peanut sauce)

On special days I wear my blankon and my sarung.

I like playing with my wayang golek.

Sometimes I play congklak.

(a board game)

On special days we have balap karung.

(sack races)

enam 6

tujuh 7

delapan 8

sembilan 9

sepuluh 10

My name is **Sophia**.
My family comes from Italy.
I speak Italian.

I love eating spaghetti bolognese

(spaghetti with minced meat sauce)

and tiramisù.

(creamy coffee-flavoured dessert)

Sometimes, I help my nonna make gnocchi.

(grandmother)

(potato dumplings)

I'm learning the tarantella.

(an Italian dance)

uno
1

due
2

tre
3

quattro
4

cinque
5

I play calcio

(football)

and nascondino.

(hide-and-seek)

Ciao!
Goodbye!

sei	sette	otto	nove	dieci
6	7	8	9	10

My name is **Emiko**.
My family comes from Japan.
I speak Japanese.

Konnichiwa!
こんにちは
Hello!

I love eating makizushi.

まきずし

(rolled sushi wrapped in seaweed)

This is my obento.

おべんとう

(boxed lunch)

On special days
I wear my kimono.
きもの

(traditional dress)

I like origami.
おりがみ

(paper folding)

ichi	ni	san	shi	go
一	二	三	四	五
1	2	3	4	5

I'm learning the taiko.
たいこ

(Japanese drum)

Sayonara!
さようなら
Goodbye!

(paper sumo)

Sometimes I play kamizumo with my friends.
かみずもう

My name is **Ji-hu**.
My family comes from Korea.
I speak Korean.

Annyong!
안녕
Hello!

I love eating bulgogi
불고기

(marinated beef)

and kimchi.
김치

(spicy pickled cabbage)

On special days
I wear my **hanbok**
한복

(traditional dress)

and I play **yut nori**.
윷놀이

(four-sticks
board game)

hana	dul	set	net	daseot
하나	둘	셋	넷	다섯
1	2	3	4	5

On New Year's day I give my parents a **sebae** to wish them good health.
세배

(New Year's bow)

I learn **taekwondo**.
태권도

(a martial art)

Annyong!
안녕
Goodbye!

yeoseot 여섯 6	ilgop 일곱 7	yeodeol 여덟 8	ahop 아홉 9	yeol 열 10

My name is **Amal**.
My family comes from Lebanon.
I speak Lebanese Arabic.

I love eating **tabouleh**
تبولة

(parsley salad)

and **kaftah.**
كفتة

(minced lamb kebab)

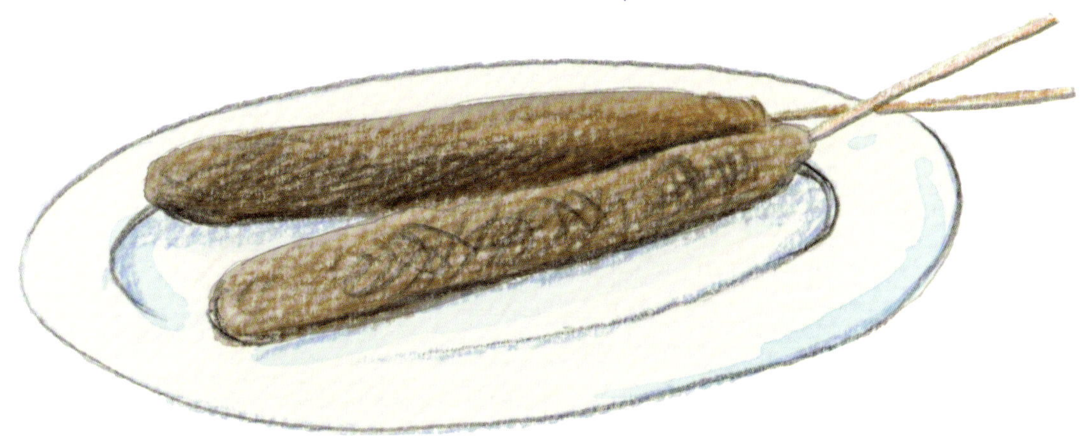

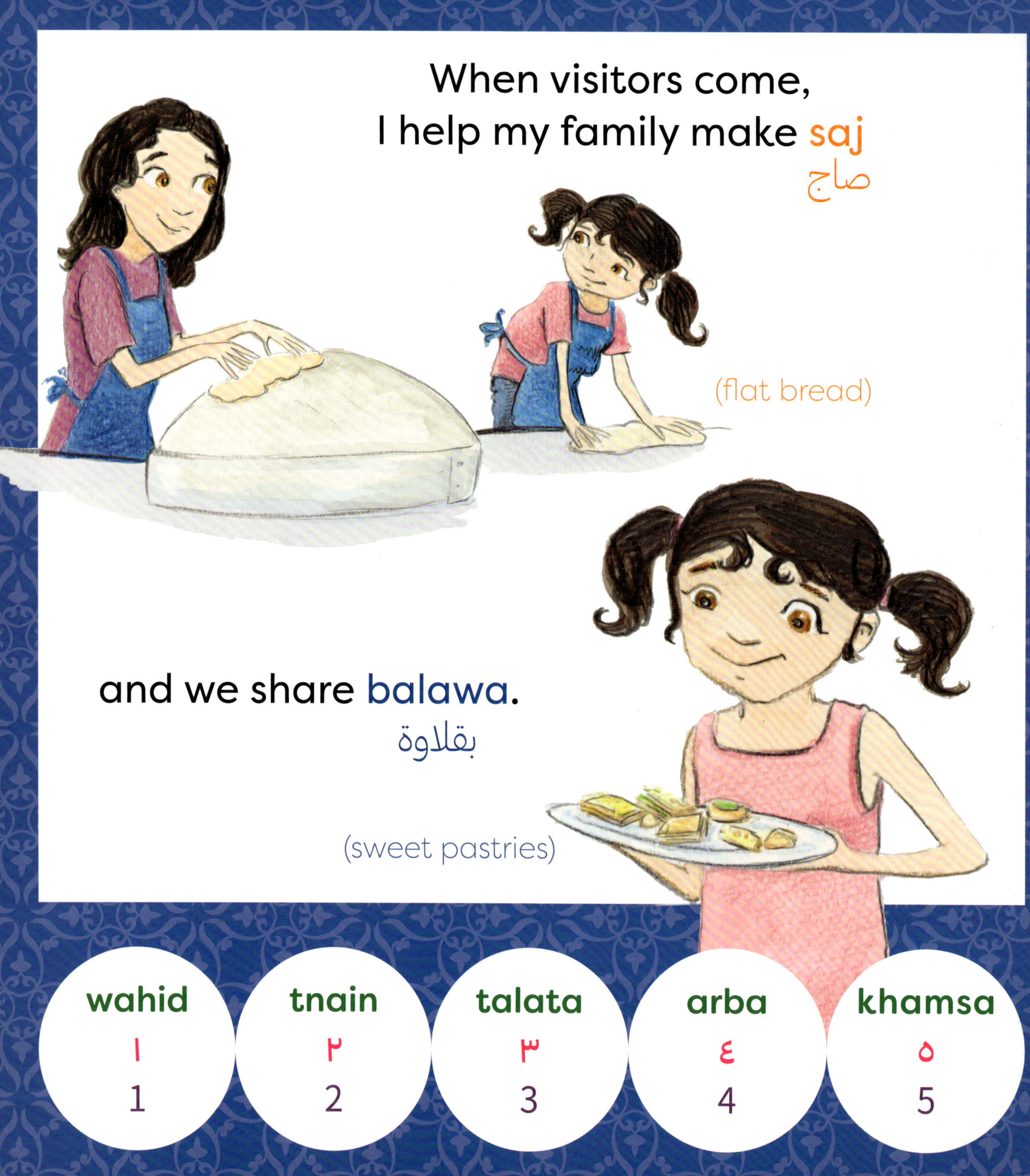

When visitors come,
I help my family make saj
صاج

(flat bread)

and we share balawa.
بقلاوة

(sweet pastries)

wahid	tnain	talata	arba	khamsa
١	٢	٣	٤	٥
1	2	3	4	5

I like playing taweleh with my jidi.

طاولة جدي

(grandfather) (backgammon)

Sometimes on special occasions I dance the dabke.

دبكة

(folk dance)

Maasalama!
مَعَ ٱلسَّلَامَة
Goodbye!

sitte	sabaah	tamane	tisa	ashara
٦	٧	٨	٩	١٠
6	7	8	9	10

My name is **Luke**.
My family comes from Tarntanya (Adelaide) in South Australia.
I speak Kaurna.

Niina marni?
Are you well?

On special days I paint ngaru on my skin. I wear a manga and I perform the palti.

Sometimes I make music with wirridla.

I play tidnaparntu

(Australian rules football)

and tantyaluparntu.

(basketball)

kuma
1

purlaityi
2

marnkutyi
3

yarapurla
4

mila
5

We go fishing in a yuku

and we catch kayinpara.

Nakutha!
See you next time!

marru	wangu	ngarla	pawa	kumirrka
6	7	8	9	10

My name is **Somsi**.
My family comes from Thailand.
I speak Thai.

Sawatdi kha!
สวัสดีค่ะ
Hello!

I love eating pad Thai
ผัดไทย

(stir-fried rice noodles)

and khao niao mamuang.
ข้าวเหนียวมะม่วง

(sticky rice and mango)

One day I'll learn to play the saw u.
ซออู้

(string instrument)

Dern kala is fun.
เดินกะลา

(a game of walking on coconut shells)

nueng	song	sam	si	ha
๑	๒	๓	๔	๕
1	2	3	4	5

On special days I perform a dance in my chut Thai.
ชุดไทย

(traditional dress)

For Mother's Day and Father's Day I make a **phuang malai**.
พวงมาลัย

(garland of flowers)

La kon kha!
ลาก่อนค่ะ
Goodbye!

My name is **Phong**.
My family comes from Vietnam.
I speak Vietnamese.

I love eating cha gio

(spring rolls)

and bun cha.

(grilled pork and noodles)

I love nhay day.

(skipping)

On special days
I wear my ao gam.

(traditional dress)

mot	hai	ba	bon	nam
1	2	3	4	5

At the Full Moon Festival I make **long den giay**

(paper lanterns)

and I sing **'Ruoc Den Thang Tam'** with my friends.

('Mid-Autumn Lantern Parade')

Tam biet!
Goodbye!

sau	bay	tam	chin	muoi
6	7	8	9	10

My name is **Pilinh**.
My family comes from Wadeye in the Northern Territory.
I speak Murrinhpatha.

I love eating ku balli and mi yidi.

We collect ku thali and cook them on the fire.

In my country I see
ku walet,
ku tek
and ku walamuma.

I am learning the nanhthi marluk.
(didgeridoo)
On special days I perform tharnpa with other boys.
(a traditional dance)
Ngurran warda!
I'm going now!
perrkenku perrkenku
4
mange numi
5

Pronunciation Guides

Welcome to the pronunciation guides for the 12 languages in *Hello!* These guides include only those sounds needed to pronounce the words used in the book and are in alphabetical order by language.

There are a few points to note before reading the guides:

- Only those consonants and consonant combinations that are pronounced differently in English are listed separately in the guides. So, if **b** is not listed, pronounce it exactly as you would a **b** in English.
- Half of the languages in this book use a non-Latin alphabet. For native English speakers, these words have been Romanised to make learning easier. For some languages, particularly Arabic dialects, there is no one correct way to Romanise words.
- There is a vowel sound (called a **schwa** in linguistics) that is difficult to describe. It is found in many different languages. It doesn't really matter whether it is represented as an **a**, **e**, **i**, **o** or **u**; the sound is more or less the same. Examples in Australian English would be the **e** in sist**e**r (sist-uh) and the **a** in **a**round (uh-round). In these guides, you will see the word 'schwa' used to describe vowel sounds.
- Chinese, Thai and Vietnamese are tonal languages. A word's meaning can change radically depending on whether the pitch of the sound is high or low and where the stress in the word is. When a tonal language is written, typically there are symbols that indicate tone. Rather than using symbols, this guide includes letters after each syllable symbolising which tone to use.

Finally, if you have heard how a particular language sounds, you might find it useful to mimic the rhythms of that language. Pronounced with feeling, these words will come alive!

Editor's note: The aim of the pronunciation guides in this book is to help readers approximate the pronunciation of the foreign-language words. They have been written with the help of native speakers of the 12 languages but are not by professional linguists.

Chinese

Mandarin Chinese is a tonal language. Its four main tones are: level, rising, falling-rising and falling. These are marked in the word list with a little L, R, FR or F after each syllable.

Words

Hua^{R}	ni^{FR} hao^{FR}	shui^{FR} jiao^{FR}	zong^{F} zi^{FR}
qi^{R} pao^{R}	feng^{L} zheng^{L}	wu^{FR} shu^{F}	min^{R} jian^{L} wu^{FR} dao^{FR}
zai^{F} jian^{F}	yi^{L}	er^{F}	san^{L}
si^{F}	wu^{FR}	liu^{F}	qi^{L}
ba^{L}	jiu^{FR}	shi^{R}	

Vowels

a	like **a** in f**a**ther	s**a**n, b**a**
a	like **e** in s**e**t	zai ji**a**n
e	like **u** in f**u**r	f**e**ng zh**e**ng
(y)**i**	like **ee** in m**ee**t	n**i** hao, y**i** (**yi** = **ee**), zai j**i**an
i	schwa, barely pronounced	s**i**, sh**i**, zong z**i**
o	like **o** in l**o**ng	z**o**ng zi
(w)u	like **oo** in r**oo**m	w**u** (**wu** = **oo**) sh**u**
ao	like **ow** in c**ow**	ni h**ao**, qi p**ao**
ui	like **wee** in s**wee**p	sh**ui** jiao

In other vowel combinations, both sounds should be pronounced. For example, in **jiu**, **i** is pronounced like **ee** in m**ee**t and **u** is pronounced like **ou** in y**ou**.

Consonants

q	like **ch** in **ch**ip	**q**i pao
r	hard like an American **r**	e**r**
z	like **ds** in goo**ds**	**z**ong **z**i
zh	like **dg** in e**dg**e	feng **zh**eng

These pictures are made from paper cut-outs. They show everyday life for children in China 100 years ago. The children are eating with chopsticks and the boy is flying a kite in the shape of a colourful dragonfly.

Greek

Stress is important in Greek. It sometimes falls on the second last syllable (fousta**nel**la, souv**la**ki, **yia**sou), sometimes on the third last syllable (meloma**ka**rono) and sometimes on the last syllable (kalamatia**nos**). Numbers 1–6 and 10 have a stress on the first syllable. Numbers 7–9 have a stress on the last syllable.

Words

Nikos	yiasou	souvlaki
melomakarono	foustanella	kalamatianos
kokkina avga	Ax Kounelaki	ena
dio	tria	tessera
pente	eksi	efta
okto	enia	deka

Vowels

a	like **a** in f**a**ther	k**a**l**a**m**a**tianos
e	like **e** in s**e**t	**e**na, d**e**ka
i	like **ee** in m**ee**t	N**i**kos, souvlak**i**
o	like **o** in p**o**st	k**o**kkina avga, mel**o**makar**o**n**o**
ia	like **ya** in **ya**rn	kalamat**ia**nos, en**ia**, y**ia**sou (**yia** = **ya**)
ou	like **oo** in b**oo**t	f**ou**stanella, s**ou**vlaki

Consonants

d	like **th** in wi**th**	**d**io
g	followed by a, o and u, like **ch** in German A**ch**tung	av**g**a
r	rolled like **r** in Spanish	tesse**r**a
t	like **t** in s**t**op	pen**t**e

These Greek dancers are rehearsing by the river in Melbourne. They're wearing their traditional costumes.

Indonesian

Unlike English, Indonesian is relatively consistent in matching sounds to spellings, but there are some exceptions to this, and there are several sounds that are tricky for English-speakers. There is no stress in Indonesian and all syllables are the same length.

Words

Budi	apa kabar	nasi goreng
gado-gado	blankon	sarung
wayang golek	congklak	balap karung
selamat tinggal	satu	dua
tiga	empat	lima
enam	tujuh	delapan
sembilan	sepuluh	

Vowels

a	like **a** in f**a**ther	**a**pa k**a**b**a**r, tig**a**
e	like **e** in s**e**t	wayang gol**e**k
e	schwa	s**e**lamat
i	like **ee** in meet	nas**i**, l**i**ma
o	like **o** in p**o**t	g**o**lek, c**o**ngklak
u	like **oo** in f**oo**d	B**u**di

In a combination of two vowels, both sounds should be pronounced. For example, in d**ua**, **u** is pronounced like **oo** in f**oo**d and **a** is pronounced like **a** in f**a**ther.

Consonants

c	like **ch** in **ch**ur**ch**	**c**ongklak
h	at the end of words, like **h** in **h**at	tuju**h**
r	tongue taps mouth top (similar to the Spanish **r** in pa**r**a)	nasi go**r**eng, sa**r**ung
r	especially at the end of words, a trill	pa kaba**r**

Djajad-Rata and Santanoe are puppets. They are characters in Indonesian stories.

Italian

Stress is important in Italian. In most words, stress lies on the second last syllable (**cin**que, taran**te**lla, So**phi**a, **cal**cio, **se**i).

Words

Sophia	ciao	spaghetti bolognese
tiramisu	nonna	gnocchi
tarantella	calcio	nascondino
uno	due	tre
quattro	cinque	sei
sette	otto	nove
dieci		

Vowels

a	like **a** in f**a**ther	tir**a**misu
e	like **e** in s**e**t	s**e**tt**e**, bologn**e**s**e**
e	like **a** in s**a**y	tr**e**
i	like **ee** in m**ee**t	Sophi**a**
o	like **o** in p**o**t	**o**tt**o**
o	like **ou** in p**ou**r	n**o**ve
u	like **oo** in f**oo**t	**u**no

When two or more vowels occur in a row, both sounds should be pronounced. For example, in d**ie**ci, **i** is pronounced like **ee** in m**ee**t and **e** is pronounced like **a** in s**a**y. An exception is c**iao**, in which the **i** is not pronounced.

Consonants

c	before i or e, like **ch** in **ch**urch	**c**iao, **c**inque, die**c**i, cal**c**io
c	otherwise like **c** in **c**ar	**c**alcio
r	rolled like **r** in Spanish	ti**r**amisu, ta**r**antella
ch	like **c** in **c**ar	gnoc**ch**i
gh	like **g** in **g**oal	spa**gh**etti
gn	like **ny** in ca**ny**on	**gn**occhi, bolo**gn**ese
sc	like **sk** in **sk**ip, unless before **i** or **e**	na**sc**ondino

The men and women in the photo are dancing the tarantella in Italy, over 130 years ago.

Japanese

Most Japanese sounds exist in English or have a close equivalent. In Japanese speech, there is no stress, but you can accent sounds using pitch.

Words

Emiko	konnichiwa	makizushi	obento
kimono	origami	taiko	kamizumo
sayonara	ichi	ni	san
shi	go	roku	shichi
hachi	kyu	ju	

Vowels

a	like **u** in c**u**t	orig**a**mi, s**a**yon**a**r**a**, s**a**n
e	like **e** in p**e**t	**E**miko
i	like **i** in **i**tchy	konn**i**ch**i**wa, **i**ch**i**, sh**i**
o	like **o** in p**o**t	**o**bent**o**, kim**o**n**o**, taik**o**
u	like **oo** in f**oo**d	j**u**
u	like **oo** in l**oo**k	makiz**u**shi, kamiz**u**mo, rok**u**
ai	like **eye**	t**ai**ko

Consonants

r	between **l** and **r**	o**r**igami, sayona**r**a, **r**oku
ky	like **cu** in **cu**te	**ky**u

This Japanese woman is wearing a beautiful kimono, and setting up a display for a festival.

Kala Lagaw Ya

Kala Lagaw Ya is an Indigenous language spoken on some of the islands, including Badu Island, in the Torres Strait.

The following letters make up the Kala Lagaw Ya alphabet:
a b d dh e g i k l m n ng o oe p r s t th u w y z.

Words

Badu	Kala Lagaw Ya	midh	akul
aka	wakul	wawmeral	koedalal
suil	Gumi Rangadh	zazi	selal
Thagay	yawo	urapun	ukasar
koeyma			

Vowels

a	like **a** in m**a**m**a**	**a**k**a**, K**a**l**a** L**a**gaw Y**a**
aw	like **ow** in n**ow**	Kala Lag**aw** Ya
e	like **e** in p**e**t	s**e**lal
i	like **i** in p**i**t	m**i**dh, zaz**i**
o	like **o** in p**o**t	yaw**o**
oe	schwa	k**oe**dalal, k**oe**yma
u	like **u** in p**u**t	Bad**u**, ak**u**l, wak**u**l, **u**rap**u**n

Consonants

ng	like **ng** in si**ng**	Gumi Ra**ng**adh
dh	like **d** in wi**d**th	mi**dh**, Gumi Ranga**dh**
th	like **t** in eigh**t**h	**Th**agay

One of the beaches of Badu Island.

Kaurna

Kaurna was the language spoken by many Aboriginal people in the Adelaide region of South Australia. After the mid-1800s, many people stopped using it, but now children are learning it again.

Stress in Kaurna is always on the first syllable.

The following letters make up the Kaurna alphabet:
a aa ai au dl dlh dly dn dnh dny i ii k l lh ly m n ng nh ny p r rd rdn rdl rl rn rr rt t th ty u ui uu w y.

Words

Tarntanya
ngaru
wirridla
yuku
kuma
yarapurla
wangu
kumirrka
Kaurna
manga
tidnaparntu
kayinpara
purlaityi
mila
ngarla
niina marni
palti
tantyaluparntu
nakutha
marnkutyi
marru
pawa

Vowels

a	like **a** in m**a**m**a**	T**a**rnt**a**ny**a**, K**a**urn**a**, n**a**kuth**a**, kum**a**, kumirrk**a**
i	like **i** in s**i**t	niina marn**i**, palt**i**, kay**i**npara, purlaity**i**, marnkuty**i**
u	like **u** in p**u**t	ngar**u**, tidnaparnt**u**, y**u**k**u**, nak**u**tha, p**u**rlaityi
ai	like **ie** in p**ie**	purl**ai**tyi
au	like **ow** in t**ow**n	K**au**rna
ii	like **ee** in m**ee**t	n**ii**na marni

Consonants

k	like **c** in **c**ut or **g** in **g**ut	**K**aurna, yu**k**u, **k**umirr**k**a
p	like **p** in **p**ig or **b** in **b**ig	**p**alti, tidna**p**arntu, yara**p**urla
t	like **t** in **t**ip or **d** in **d**ip	pal**t**i
n	at the start of a word, like **n** in te**n**th	**n**iina marni, **n**akutha
ny	like **ni** in o**ni**on	Tarnta**nya**
ng	like **ng** in si**ng**	**ng**arla, wa**ng**u, ma**ng**a
rl	like **l** in **l**og but with tongue tip curled slightly back	pu**rl**aityi, nga**rl**a
rn	like **n** in **n**od but with tongue tip curled slightly back	Ta**rn**tanya, Kau**rn**a
rr	rolled like **r** in Spanish	wi**rr**idla, ma**rr**u, kumi**rr**ka
t	at the start of a word, like **d** in wi**d**th	**t**idnaparntu, **T**arntanya
th	like **d** in wi**d**th	naku**th**a
ty	like **ch** in **ch**urch	tan**ty**aluparntu, marnku**ty**i

Korean

Most of the Korean sounds exist in English or have a close equivalent. In Korean speech, there is no stress.

Words

Ji-hu
hanbok
hana
daseot
ahop
annyong
yut nori
dul
yeoseot
yeol
bulgogi
sebae
set
ilgop
kimchi
taekwondo
net
yeodeol

Vowels

a	like **a** in f**a**ther	**a**nnyong
e	like **e** in s**e**t	s**e**bae, s**e**t, n**e**t
i	like **ee** in m**ee**t	J**i**-hu, k**i**mch**i**
o	like **o** in p**o**re	taekwond**o,** bulg**o**gi, hanb**o**k, ilg**o**p
o	like **u** in s**u**n	taekw**o**ndo
u	like **oo** in t**oo**	b**u**lgogi, y**u**t nori, Ji-h**u**
ae	like **a** in p**a**y	seb**ae**, t**ae**kwondo
eo	like **u** in y**ou**ng	y**eo**s**eo**t, y**eo**d**eo**l, y**eo**l

Consonants

r	between **l** and **d** (similar to the Spanish **r** in pa**r**a)	yut no**r**i

In Korea, the tiger is a gentle creature who brings good luck and protects people against evil spirits.

Lebanese Arabic

Arabic has many different dialects and is the official language in more than 22 countries. The Arabic taught in schools is different to the Arabic spoken in homes and on the streets. This guide is for Lebanese Arabic as spoken on the streets of Beirut, the capital city of Lebanon, where Amal's family comes from.

The apostrophe in some words tells you to pause before continuing with the next sound.

Words

Amal	marhaba	tabouleh	kaftah
saj	ba'lawa	taweleh	jidi
dabke	ma'asalama	wahid	tnain
talata	arba	khamsa	sitte
sabaah	tamane	tisa	'ashara

Vowels

a	like **u** in **u**p	marh**a**b**a**, t**a**mane, **'**ash**a**ra, kh**a**msa, d**a**bke, k**a**ft**a**h
a	like **e** in s**e**t	tal**a**t**a**, khams**a**, b**a'**l**a**wa, ma'asal**a**m**a**
a	like **a** in f**a**ther	**A**mal, m**a**rhaba, m**a'a**salama, **a**rb**a**, tis**a**, ba'law**a**
a	like **a** in m**a**re	tam**a**ne
a	like **au** in s**au**sage	s**a**j
e	like **e** in s**e**t	taboul**e**h, wah**i**d, dabk**e**, taman**e**
i	like **i** in s**i**t	j**i**di, s**i**tte
i	like **ee** in m**ee**t	jid**i**
ou	like **oo** in f**oo**d	tab**ou**leh

Consonants

j	like **g** in carria**g**e (with a short buzz)	**j**idi
r	rolled breathily (similar to the Spanish **r** in pa**r**a)	ma**r**haba
w	like **w** in **w**in	ba'la**wa**
kh	breathy guttural sound (like lightly clearing your throat)	**kh**amsa

Double consonants are usually separated with a pause; for example, si**tt**e.

This photo of the Middle Eastern Nights Band was taken at a Lebanese festival in Melbourne.

Murrinhpatha

The Aboriginal people of Wadeye, on the west coast of the Nothern Territory, speak Murrinhpatha.

The following letters make up the Murrinhpatha alphabet:
a b d dh e g i k l m n nh ng p r rd rl rn rr rt t th u w y.

Words

Pilinh	Wadeye	Murrinhpatha
nhinhi-ka patha thanam	ku balli	mi yidi
ku thali	ku walet	ku tek
ku walamuma	nanhthi marluk	tharnpa
ngurran warda	numi	perrkenku
perrkenkuneme	perrkenku perrkenku	mange numi

Vowels

a	like **u** in n**u**t	ku w**a**let, m**a**nge numi
e	like **e** in p**e**n	p**e**rrk**e**nkun**e**m**e**
i	like **i** in k**i**t	ku thal**i**, m**i** y**i**d**i**
u	like **u** in p**u**t	n**u**mi, k**u** walam**u**m**a**

Consonants

ng	like **ng** in si**ng**	**ng**urran warda
nh	like **n** in **n**ews	na**nh**thi marluk, **nh**i**nh**i-ka
ll	double length (like **ll** in Italian be**ll**a)	ku ba**ll**i
rd	like **d** in **d**og but with tongue tip curled slightly back	ngurran wa**rd**a
rl	like **l** in **l**og but with tongue tip curled slightly back	nanhthi ma**rl**uk
rn	like **n** in **n**o but with tongue tip curled slightly back	tha**rn**pa
rr	rolled like **r** in Spanish	pe**rr**kenku
th	like **t** in eigh**th**	**th**ali
th	like **tch** in ca**tch**	nanh**thi**, **th**arnpa

It's hot in the country around Wadeye but there are rivers to swim in.

Thai

Thai is a tonal language that uses five pitches: falling, rising, high, mid and low. To be understood, you must pronounce each syllable using the correct tone. These are marked in the word list with a little F, R, H, M or L after each syllable.

Some vowels in Thai are longer than others. Examples of a long **a** can be found in kh**a** and h**a**. The a in p**a**d Thai is short.

Words

Somsi
khao^{F} niao^{R} mamuang^{F}
chut^{H} Thai^{M}
nueng^{L}
si^{L}
jet^{L}
sip^{L}

sa^{L}wat^{L}di^{M} kha^{F}
saw^{M} u^{F}
phuang^{M} ma^{M}lai^{M}
song^{R}
ha^{F}
paet^{L}

pad^{L} Thai^{M}
dern^{M} ka^{L}la^{M}
la^{M} kon^{L} kha^{F}
sam^{R}
hok^{L}
kao^{F}

Vowels

a	like **a** in f**a**ther	s**a**w**a**tdi kh**a**, khao niao m**a**muang, s**a**m, h**a**, dern k**a**l**a**, l**a** kon kha
e	like **e** in s**e**t	j**e**t
e	like **u** in f**u**r	d**e**rn kala
i	like **ee** in m**ee**t	Soms**i**, sawatd**i** kha, s**i**
i	like **i** in h**i**p	s**i**p
o	like **o** in n**o**te	S**o**msi, h**o**k
o	like **aw** in s**aw**	s**o**ng, la k**o**n kha
u	like **u** in p**u**t	ch**u**t Thai
u	like **oo** in b**oo**t	saw **u**
ae	like **a** in h**a**nd	p**ae**t
ai	like **i** in h**i**	pad Th**ai**, phuang mal**ai**
ao	like **ow** in c**ow**	kh**ao** niao mamuang, k**ao**
iao	like **iao** in m**iao**w	khao n**iao** mamuang
ue	schwa	n**ue**ng

In other vowel combinations, both sounds should be pronounced. For example, in mam**ua**ng, **u** is pronounced like **oo** in m**oo** and **a** is pronounced like **a** in c**a**r.

Consonants

d	between **d** and **t**	pa**d** Thai
k	like **g** in **g**et	**k**ala, **k**ao
ch	like **ch** in **ch**ip	**ch**ut
kh	like **k** in **k**iss	**kh**a, **kh**ao
ph	like **p** in **p**et	**ph**uang
th	like **t** in **t**ime	**Th**ai

There are hundreds of different Thai dances. The dancers wear beautiful costumes.

Vietnamese

Vietnamese is a tonal language. It has 12 vowels, which can be pronounced using six tones, turning them into 72 distinct vowels. For example, the word ma can mean horse, ghost, mother and other things depending on the tone used!

The six tones in Vietnamese are: level, hanging (low gradual falling), sharp (middle gradual rising), asking (middle low middle), tumbling (rising falling rising) and heavy (middle sharp falling). These are marked in the word list with a little L, H, S, A, T or H after each syllable. There is also a regional difference in how words are pronounced in the north and in the south. Phong's family comes from South Vietnam.

The little symbols over some vowels in the word list change the meaning and tell you how to pronounce the letter.

Words

Phong
nhay^{A} dây^{L}
Thang^{S} Tam^{S}
ba^{L}
bây^{A}

xin^{L} chao^{H}
ao^{S} gâm^{S}
tam^{H} biêt^{H}
bôn^{S}
tam^{S}

cha^{A} gio^{H}
lông^{H} đen^{H} giây^{S}
môt^{H}
năm^{L}
chin^{S}

bun^{S} cha^{A}
Rươc^{S} Đen^{A}
hai^{L}
sau^{S}
mươi^{H}

Vowels

a	like **a** in f**a**ther	ch**a** gio, b**a**, Rươc Đen Th**a**ng T**a**m
â	like **u** in b**u**t	nhay d**â**y, ao g**â**m, lông đen gi**â**y
ă	like **a** in h**a**t	n**ă**m
e ê	like **e** in s**e**t	lông đ**e**n giây, tam bi**ê**t
i	like **i** in b**i**t	x**i**n chao, mươ**i**
o	like **o** in p**o**t	cha gi**o**
ô	like **o** in p**o**st	l**ô**ng đen giây, m**ô**t, b**ô**n
ơ	like **u** in f**u**r	mư**ơ**i, Rư**ơ**c Đen Thang Tam
ư	like **oo** in b**oo**t	m**ư**ơi, R**ư**ơc Đen Thang Tam
y	like **ee** in m**ee**t	nha**y** dây, lông đen giâ**y**
ai	like **i** in h**i**gh	h**ai**
ao	like **ow** in n**ow**	xin ch**ao**
au	like **ow** in n**ow**	s**au**

In other vowel combinations, both sounds should be pronounced. For example, in b**iê**t, **i** is pronounced like **ee** in m**ee**t and **ê** is pronounced like **e** in s**e**t.

Consonants

d	like **y** in **y**ou	nhay **d**ây
đ (Đ)	like **d** in **d**og	lông **đ**en giây
g	like **g** in **g**ood	ao **g**âm
r	like **r** in **r**ing	**R**ươc Đen Thang Tam
t	like **t** in s**t**op	**t**am
x	like **s** in **s**un	**x**in chao
ch	like **ch** in **ch**op	bun **ch**a, **ch**in
gi	like **y** in **y**ou	cha **gi**o, lông đen **gi**ây
nh	like **ny** in ca**ny**on	**nh**ay dây
ph	like **ph** in **ph**one	**Ph**ong
th	like **t** in **t**op	Rươc Đen **Th**ang Tam